Article 40

Child Criminal Justice

A Commentary on the United Nations Convention
on the Rights of the Child

Editors

André Alen, Johan Vande Lanotte, Eugeen Verhellen,
Fiona Ang, Eva Berghmans and Mieke Verheyde

Article 40

Child Criminal Justice

By

Geraldine Van Bueren

Barrister and Professor of International Human Rights Law in
Queen Mary, University of London and in the University of Cape Town

MARTINUS NIJHOFF PUBLISHERS
LEIDEN • BOSTON
2006

This book is printed on acid-free paper.

A Cataloging-in-Publication record for this book is available from the Library of Congress.

Cite as: G. Van Bueren, "Article 40: Child Criminal Justice", in: A. Alen, J. Vande Lanotte, E. Verhellen, F. Ang, E. Berghmans and M. Verheyde (Eds.) *A Commentary on the United Nations Convention on the Rights of the Child* (Martinus Nijhoff Publishers, Leiden, 2006).

ISSN 1574-8626
ISBN 90-04-14888-4

Cover image by Nadia, 1 1/2 years old

http://www.brill.nl

PRINTED IN THE NETHERLANDS

CONTENTS

LIST OF ABBREVIATIONS

African Children's Charter	African Charter on the Rights and Welfare of the Child
American Convention	American Convention on Human Rights
Beijing Commentary	Commentary to Beijing Rules
Beijing Rules	UN Standard Minimum Rules for the Administration of Juvenile Justice
CCPR	International Covenant on Civil and Political Rights
CEDAW	International Convention on the Elimination of All Forms of Discrimination against Women
CERD	International Convention on the Elimination of All Forms of Racial Discrimination
CESCR	International Covenant on Economic, Social and Cultural Rights
CESCR Committee	UN Committee on Economic, Social and Cultural Rights
CRC	International Convention on the Rights of the Child
CRC Committee	UN Committee on the Rights of the Child
ECHR	European Convention on Human Rights
ECmHR	European Commission on Human Rights
ECOSOC	UN Economic and Social Council
ECtHR	European Court of Human Rights
EU	European Union
Guidelines	UN Guidelines for Action on Children in the Criminal Justice System
Human Rights Committee	UN Committee on Civil and Political Rights
NGO	Non-governmental Organization
UN	United Nations
UNDP	United Nations Development Programme
UNESCO	United Nations Educational, Scientific and Cultural Organisation
UNICEF	United Nations Children's Fund

AUTHOR BIOGRAPHY

Geraldine Van Bueren is Professor of International Human Rights Law at Queen Mary, University of London, and was appointed to a second concurrent chair at the University of Cape Town in 2001. She is also the Director of the Programme on International Rights of the Child at Queen Mary's.

In 2003 she was awarded the Child Rights Lawyer Award. The Award, jointly organized by the Law Society, UNICEF and The Lawyer, honours lawyers who have done outstanding work in the field of children's rights.

Geraldine Van Bueren is a barrister and an Associate Tenant with Doughty Street Chambers. Goodenough College has appointed her as a Fellow.

Professor Geraldine Van Bueren is one of the original drafters of the United Nations Convention on the Rights of the Child.

She also helped draft the United Nations Rules for the Protection of Juveniles Deprived of their Liberty, the UNHCR Guidelines on Refugee Children and the United Nations Programme of Action on Children in the Criminal Justice System. She works extensively with intergovernmental organisations, governments and non-governmental organisations raising national laws to the international legal standard, including the United Nations, the Commonwealth, Save the Children and Human Rights Watch. She represented Amnesty International for ten years at the UN on children's rights and is a member of the Advisory Board of Human Rights Watch (Children's Rights Project).

Recent publications include: International Law on the Rights of the Child (Kluwer, 1998); International Documents on Children 2nd edn (Kluwer, 1998); Childhood Abused: Protecting Children Against Torture, Inhuman and Degrading Treatment and Punishment (Aldershot, Dartmouth, 1998). Her writings have been cited in courts around the world, most recently by the English House of Lords, the Constitutional Court of South Africa and the European Court of Human Rights.

TEXT OF ARTICLE 40

ARTICLE 40

1. States Parties recognize the right of every child alleged as, accused of, or recognized as having infringed the penal law to be treated in a manner consistent with the promotion of the child's sense of dignity and worth, which reinforces the child's respect for the human rights and fundamental freedoms of others and which takes into account the child's age and the desirability of promoting the child's reintegration and the child's assuming a constructive role in society.

2. To this end and having regard to the relevant provisions of international instruments, States Parties shall, in particular, ensure that:

(a) No child shall be alleged as, be accused of, or recognized as having infringed the penal law by reason of acts or omissions that were not prohibited by national or international law at the time they were committed;

(b) Every child alleged as or accused of having infringed the penal law has at least the following guarantees:
(i) To be presumed innocent until proven guilty according to law;

ARTICLE 40

1. Les Etats parties reconnaissent à tout enfant suspecté, accusé ou convaincu d'infraction à la loi pénale le droit à un traitement qui soit de nature à favoriser son sens de la dignité et de la valeur personnelle, qui renforce son respect pour les droits de l'homme et les libertés fondamentales d'autrui, et qui tienne compte de son âge ainsi que de la nécessité de faciliter sa réintégration dans la société et de lui faire assumer un rôle constructif au sein de celle-ci.

2. A cette fin, et compte tenu des dispositions pertinentes des instruments internationaux, les Etats parties veillent en particulier :

a) A ce qu'aucun enfant ne soit suspecté, accusé ou convaincu d'infraction à la loi pénale en raison d'actions ou d'omissions qui n'étaient pas interdites par le droit national ou international au moment où elles ont été commises;

b) A ce que tout enfant suspecté ou accusé d'infraction à la loi pénale ait au moins le droit aux garanties suivantes :
i) Etre présumé innocent jusqu'à ce que sa culpabilité ait été légalement établie;

(ii) To be informed promptly and directly of the charges against him or her, and, if appropriate, through his or her parents or legal guardians and to have legal or other appropriate assistance in the preparation and presentation of his or her defence;

(iii) To have the matter determined without delay by a competent, independent and impartial authority or judicial body in a fair hearing according to law, in the presence of legal or other appropriate assistance and, unless it is considered not to be in the best interest of the child, in particular, taking into account his or her age or situation, his or her parents or legal guardians;

(iv) Not to be compelled to give testimony or to confess guilt; to examine or have examined adverse witnesses and to obtain the participation and examination of witnesses on his or her behalf under conditions of equality;

(v) If considered to have infringed the penal law, to have this decision and any measures imposed in consequence thereof reviewed by a higher competent, independent and impartial authority or judicial body according to law;

(vi) To have the free assistance of an interpreter if the child cannot understand or speak the language used;

ii) Etre informé dans le plus court délai et directement des accusations portées contre lui, ou, le cas échéant, par l'intermédiaire de ses parents ou représentants légaux, et bénéficier d'une assistance juridique ou de toute autre assistance appropriée pour la préparation et la présentation de sa défense;

iii) Que sa cause soit entendue sans retard par une autorité ou une instance judiciaire compétentes, indépendantes et impartiales, selon une procédure équitable aux termes de la loi, en présence de son conseil juridique ou autre et, à moins que cela ne soit jugé contraire à l'intérêt supérieur de l'enfant en raison notamment de son âge ou de sa situation, en présence de ses parents ou représentants légaux;

iv) Ne pas être contraint de témoigner ou de s'avouer coupable; interroger ou faire interroger les témoins à charge, et obtenir la comparution et l'interrogatoire des témoins à décharge dans des conditions d'égalité;

v) S'il est reconnu avoir enfreint la loi pénale, faire appel de cette décision et de toute mesure arrêtée en conséquence devant une autorité ou une instance judiciaire supérieure compétentes, indépendantes et impartiales, conformément à la loi;

vi) Se faire assister gratuitement d'un interprète s'il ne comprend ou ne parle pas la langue utilisée;

(vii) To have his or her privacy fully respected at all stages of the proceedings

3. States Parties shall seek to promote the establishment of laws, procedures, authorities and institutions specifically applicable to children alleged as, accused of, or recognized as having infringed the penal law, and, in particular:

(a) The establishment of a minimum age below which children shall be presumed not to have the capacity to infringe the penal law;

(b) Whenever appropriate and desirable, measures for dealing with such children without resorting to judicial proceedings, providing that human rights and legal safeguards are fully respected.

4. A variety of dispositions, such as care, guidance and supervision orders; counselling; probation; foster care; education and vocational training programmes and other alternatives to institutional care shall be available to ensure that children are dealt with in a manner appropriate to their well-being and proportionate both to their circumstances and the offence.

vii) Que sa vie privée soit pleinement respectée à tous les stades de la procédure.

3. Les Etats parties s'efforcent de promouvoir l'adoption de lois, de procédures, la mise en place d'autorités et d'institutions spécialement conçues pour les enfants suspectés, accusés ou convaincus d'infraction à la loi pénale, et en particulier :

a) D'établir un âge minimum au-dessous duquel les enfants seront présumés n'avoir pas la capacité d'enfreindre la loi pénale;

b) De prendre des mesures, chaque fois que cela est possible et souhaitable, pour traiter ces enfants sans recourir à la procédure judiciaire, étant cependant entendu que les droits de l'homme et les garanties légales doivent être pleinement respectés.

4. Toute une gamme de dispositions, relatives notamment aux soins, à l'orientation et à la supervision, aux conseils, à la probation, au placement familial, aux programmes d'éducation générale et professionnelle et aux solutions autres qu'institutionnelles seront prévues en vue d'assurer aux enfants un traitement conforme à leur bien-être et proportionné à leur situation et à l'infraction.

CHAPTER ONE

INTRODUCTION

1. Overview

1. Upon adoption of the Convention on the Rights of the Child[1] there was much rejoicing at the potential of Article 40 to transform child justice systems, which were still governed by the punitive, to those more closely aligned to the family court principles of the best interests of the child. However, the response of States has been more akin to a stop-go policy rather than wholesale transformation.

2. The CRC Committee decided to devote 13th November 1995 as a 'Discussion Day' on the administration of child criminal justice. This initiative reflected the Committee's concern that the general principles of the Convention were not being adequately reflected in national legislation or practice.[2] The Committee's request for a holistic approach to be taken to child criminal justice was highlighted in the 1997 Guidelines for Action on Children in the Criminal Justice System.[3] It calls on those involved in child criminal justice to act in accordance with four of the general principles of the Convention: non-discrimination (including gender sensitivity), the best interests of the child, the child's right to life, survival and development, and respect for the views of the child.[4] The Guidelines also refer to the need to adopt a rights-based orientation to child criminal justice and a holistic approach to implementation through maximisation of resources and efforts.[5]

3. Progress has been made at the formal level in the creation of juvenile courts in countries where none existed prior to the Convention, and in the expansion, in some states, of diversions. Yet the quiet revolution[6] in child

---

[1] UN Convention on the Rights of the Child 1989 (hereinafter: CRC).
[2] CRC Committee, *Day of General Discussion: The administration of juvenile justice* (UN Doc. CRC/C/43 Annex VIII, 1995)(hereinafter: CRC Committee, *Day of General Discussion*), para. 218.
[3] Guidelines for Action on Children in the Criminal Justice System, recommended by ECOSOC resolution 1997/30 of 21 July 1997 (hereinafter: Guidelines for Action).
[4] Guidelines for Action 8(a).
[5] Guidelines for Action 8(b) and (c).
[6] G. Van Bueren, *The International Law on the Rights of the Child* (The Hague, Martinus Nijhoff Publishers, 1998), p. 169.

criminal justice still remains to a major extent unheralded. An analysis of the concluding observations to the CRC Committee with respect to child criminal justice between 1993 and 2000 revealed that out of the 141 reports considered, twenty-one States were asked to undertake a comprehensive reform of their child criminal justice system.

4. This is in part because the CRC Committee and other international bodies have yet to respond adequately to the genuine concern expressed by some governments who regard themselves as being unable to afford universal child education and health services and therefore believe themselves unable to devote sufficient scarce resources for a minority of children who are in the child criminal justice system.

The CRC Committee recognizes the limited resources of States and is aware of the threat that this presents to the development of an effective child criminal justice system. In its concluding observations on the report of Sierra Leone, the Committee, while recognizing the limited resources available, expressed concern over the lack of clear policy on the allocation of resources in favour of children.[7] With particular regard to child criminal justice, it called on the State Party to make every effort to gather information on the numbers of children in detention and to make use of alternatives to imprisonment.[8] The absence of information for policies and the lack of efforts to make policy will rarely be defensible on account of lack of resources.

States do risk losing public confidence if they seek to attain the standards set out in the relevant international instruments on the administration of child criminal justice without appreciating the social costs of implementation.[9] It is for this reason that the CRC Committee has consistently recommended that State Parties seek technical assistance from those international and non-governmental organisations which mostly now make up the Co-ordination Panel on Technical Advice and Assistance on Juvenile Justice.[10] The stress which the Committee places on international co-oper-

---

[7] CRC Committee, *Concluding Observations: Sierra Leone* (UN Doc. CRC/C/15/Add.116, 2000), para 14.

[8] *Ibid.*, para. 91.

[9] See J. Sloth-Nielsen, 'The Contribution of Children's Rights to the Reconstruction of Society: Some Implications for the Constitutionalisation of Children's Rights in South Africa', *The International Journal of Children's Rights* 4, No. 4, 1996, p. 323.

[10] The International Network on Juvenile Justice listed 100 States that had received such a recommendation from the Committee up until 2002. The bodies making up the panel are the Office of the High Commissioner for Human Rights, the Centre for International Crime Prevention, UNDP, UNICEF and the International Network on Juvenile Justice.

ation and technical assistance reflects the priority which the UN system has placed on child criminal justice. There is a recognized need for different international, regional and non-governmental organisations to co-operate in areas of research, training, dissemination and exchange of information, implementation and monitoring of existing systems, as well as in specific programmes of technical assistance.[11] The Coordination Panel has the considerable task of ensuring that finite resources are used in the most effective manner.

The UN Guidelines for Action on Children in the Criminal Justice System call for a strategy to set out how the Panel should be used to activate further international co-operation in the field of child criminal justice.[12] The Panel's aim is to assist in the identification of common problems, compile examples of good practice and analyse shared experience. In doing so, it is foreseen that it will help to develop a more strategic approach to needs assessment and to effective proposals for action.[13] Projects taken on by the bodies making up the Coordination Panel were referred to in the report of the Secretary-General on the 'Use and application of the UN standards and norms, especially concerning juvenile justice and penal reform'.[14]

One of the extraordinary but unchallenged extensions of the UN Committee's mandate is in relation to the legal force it ascribes to the three sets of UN Rules. Rather than seeing them as mainly non-binding *per se*, States appear to have accepted without comment the application of the rules to the child criminal justice system. The European Court of Human Rights has adopted a different approach, one perhaps which it regards as more in keeping with its judicial function. For the European Court of Human Rights an action based solely on the violation of one of the rules, which is not a reflection of one of the articles of the European Convention on Human Rights, will fail.

---

[11] CRC Committee, *Day of General Discussion* (note 2), para. 223–224. The need to further strengthen international cooperation and practical technical assistance was recognized in ECOSOC Resolution 1996/13, 23rd July 1996 and in ECOSOC Resolution 1997/30, 21st July 1997.

[12] See Guidelines for Action 34–40.

[13] Commission on Crime Prevention and Criminal Justice, *Reform of the criminal justice system: Use and application of standards and norms, especially concerning juvenile justice and penal reform* (UN Doc. E/CN.15/2002/3, 2002), paras. 49–64.

[14] *Ibid.*

2. *History*

5. The incorporation of specific rights of children into the administration of juvenile justice is a comparatively recent development in the international law on the rights of children The 1924 Declaration on the Rights of the Child recognized that 'the delinquent child must be reclaimed'. However, the 1959 Declaration contained no provision on the protection of the child in conflict with the law. Italy had attempted to include a specific provision on the administration of juvenile justice in the 1959 Declaration on the Rights of the Child but this had failed.

6. It was not until the International Covenant on Civil and Political Rights[15] that specific provisions regulating the administration of juvenile justice were enshrined in a global treaty, but these were concerned with specific necessary improvements rather than a move towards child centred criminal justice systems.

The provisions found in Article 10(2)(b) provide for the separation of accused juveniles from adults and for their speedy adjudication, and Article 14(4) provides that the trial procedures for juveniles should take account of the age of juveniles and the desirability of promoting their rehabilitation.

7. As an increasing number of States began to develop separate juvenile justice systems, so the need became apparent on the international level for a complete framework which States could utilize for guidance in establishing and operating their own national juvenile justice systems.

8. In 1980, the Sixth UN Congress on the Prevention of Crime and the Treatment of Offenders called for the preparation of minimum rules regulating the administration of juvenile justice. In 1985, appropriately on Human Rights Day, the General Assembly adopted the UN Standard Minimum Rules for the Administration of Juvenile Justice, known as the Beijing Rules.[16] They provide, as intended, a framework within which a national juvenile justice system should operate and a model for States of a fair and humane response to juveniles who may find themselves in conflict with the law.

The Beijing Rules, which are divided into six parts, cover the entire juvenile justice processes: General Principles; Investigation and Prosecution; Adjudication and Disposition; Non-institutional treatment; Institutional

---

[15] International Covenant on Civil and Political Rights 1966 (hereinafter: CCPR).
[16] UN Standard Minimum Rules for the Administration of Juvenile Justice, adopted by General Assembly resolution 40/33 of 29 November 1985 (hereinafter: Beijing Rules).

Treatment and Research and Planning; Policy Formulation; and Evaluation. It is an over-simplification to conclude that because the Beijing Rules are not a treaty they are as an entire body of Rules non-binding *per se*. Some of the Rules have become binding on States Parties by being incorporated into the CRC, others can be treated not as establishing new rights but as providing more detail on the contents of existing rights. The latter is an approach which is not unique to juvenile justice and has already been adopted by the Human Rights Committee in relation to prisoners' rights.

Although not a binding instrument *per se* and therefore having no monitoring body, there was an attempt at creating scope for monitoring the implementation of the Beijing Rules. Item 7 of the resolution to which the Beijing Rules are attached, invites States to inform the Secretary-General on the implementation of the Rules and to report regularly to the Committee on Crime Prevention and Control on the results achieved. The Rules also provide, at the request of a State, for the assistance of the Secretary-General in adapting legislation and policies and in the development of alternatives to institutionalisation. Such a service was made available because the Rules recognize in the Preamble that existing legislation and policies may require review and amendment in light of the standards enshrined in the Beijing Rules. States are also requested to provide the necessary resources to ensure the successful implementation of the Rules, and non-governmental organisations are urged to 'collaborate' to implement the principles. In other words the General Assembly is seeking to overcome the handicap of the standards being adopted as recommendatory by advising on methods of implementation. In the first report of the Secretary-General on the implementation of the Rules, the Bahamas, Burundi, Chad and Peru reported that implementation had been delayed or was not feasible owing to a lack of resources. They requested the technical and financial assistance to facilitate juvenile justice reform which the Rules envisaged.

9. The Beijing Rules were adopted by the General Assembly whilst the CRC was being drafted. Hence, the drafters of the Convention had the opportunity of raising the existing binding standards regulating the administration of juvenile justice. In 1988 however, at the completion of the first reading of the CRC, the draft article which focuses on the administration of juvenile justice did little more than insert the word 'child' into existing international standards. During the second reading of the Convention, the article on the administration of juvenile justice was significantly revised.

Although the CRC is a holistic treaty, there are two other key articles on child criminal justice: Article 37 and Article 39.

CHAPTER TWO

COMPARISON WITH RELATED INTERNATIONAL
HUMAN RIGHTS PROVISIONS

10. As with other articles of the Convention, many of the provisions enshrined in Article 40 are *de novo*. These include minimum age, the emphasis on diversions, and the promotion of the child's sense of dignity and worth as a fundamental principle of the child criminal justice system.

11. Everything hinges on the definitions of juvenile and child and the relationship between them. Although the Human Rights Committee has observed that under the CCPR the limits of 'juvenile age' are to be determined by 'each State Party in the light of relevant social, cultural and other conditions', the Committee itself 'is of the opinion that all individuals under the age of 18 should be treated as juveniles' at least in matters relating to criminal justice.[17]

The CRC Committee has taken the approach that the duties on States Parties enshrined in Article 40 apply to all children up to majority, regardless of whether the national criminal law treats them as if they were adult. So far, this is an approach which has not met with any resistance by the States Parties.

As a means of fulfilling the aims of child criminal justice enshrined in international law, Article 40(3) of the CRC provides that States Parties should seek,

> 'to promote the establishment of laws, procedures, authorities and institutions specifically applicable to children [...]'

This is an important addition to the protection of the rights of children who are accused of being in conflict with the law as Article 14(4) of the CCPR is far more limited and only provides that procedures concerning juveniles should 'take into account their age and the desirability of promoting rehabilitation'.

---

[17] Human Rights Committee, *General Comment No. 9: Humane treatment of persons deprived of their liberty (Art. 10)*(UN Doc. A147/40, 1982).

The duty is wide ranging, arising from the earliest moment of the allegation, and focuses not only on the establishment of the necessary legal framework, but also on the need for specific child criminal justice authorities, procedures and institutions. This includes specially trained law enforcement personnel.

The duty under the CRC, however, is only 'to seek to promote' which is regrettably weaker than the corresponding and earlier duty under the American Convention on Human Rights which is a stricter and more direct duty to bring accused children before specialized tribunals.

12. The African Charter on the Rights and Welfare of the Child which was adopted a year later than its UN counterpart has its specific child criminal justice provisions enshrined in Articles 17 and 30. It does not incorporate an express provision obliging States to establish specialized child criminal justice institutions and personnel.

13. All the States Parties to the regional human rights children's rights treaties are party to the CRC. It is possible therefore to read Article 40 into the regional provisions. This is important as the CRC still regrettably lacks a petitioning mechanism[18] and so relief for children for violations is only indirect through reporting and special rapporteur mechanisms. However, both the American Convention and the two African Charters allow for the possibility of children petitioning for direct remedies for violations of their child criminal justice entitilments.

14. Although the CRC is a major progressive step towards a child-centred criminal justice system, the CCPR does provide additional safeguards for children.

One of the reasons for the additional protections is that there is an inherent tension in Article 40. On the one hand, Article 40 seeks to establish a child centred criminal justice system focussing on the child's welfare which is not necessarily one safeguarded by lawyers, and on the other hand, the Convention recognizes that traditional juvenile justice is dependant upon lawyers. The results of this tension is that Article 40 does not reiterate all the legal protections found in other treaties, particularly all of those found in the CCPR. There is, for example, no repetition of the rule against double

---

[18] See Art. 6(5) CCPR. See also the call for an international petitioning system in G. Van Bueren, *o.c* (note 6), p. 410. On behalf of Amnesty International the author proposed that an international petitioning scheme should be included in the CRC, but her proposal attracted insufficient support.

jeopardy, separation of convicted and unconvicted children,[19] the prohibition on the imposition of a heavier penalty and the opportunity for offenders to benefit from lighter penalties,[20] or an entitlement for compensation for child victims of miscarriages of justice.[21]

Article 14(3)(a) of the CCPR provides that everyone should be informed not only promptly of any charges but also 'in detail' in a language which enables them to understand the 'nature and the cause' of the charge. According to the Human Rights Committee, the right to be informed of the charge applies to all cases concerning criminal charges, regardless of whether the person is in detention, and the right to be informed 'promptly' requires that the information is provided by the competent authority 'as soon as the charge is first made'.

As far as children are concerned, the right to be informed in detail in a language which enables children to understand the nature of the charges against them places a duty on the State Party not only to use a language which the child understands, but also to communicate the information in a manner which a child is capable of understanding.

Under Article 14(3)(b) of the CCPR, children are entitled to have adequate time and facilities for the preparation of their defence and to communicate with counsel of their own choosing. What constitutes adequate time will depend on the circumstances of each individual child's case. Adequate facilities for the preparation of a defence include access to documents, to other material evidence and to counsel. The right of the child to 'legal or other appropriate assistance' enshrined in the CRC will depend upon the nature of a State's legal procedures for breaching the penal law. The CRC Committee has observed that access to legal and other assistance and free legal aid were often not available to accused children.[22] The Guidelines for Action on Children in the Criminal Justice System call for priority to be given to setting up agencies and programmes to provide legal and other assistance to children, if needed free of charge.[23]

15. Whatever the type of proceeding, children are entitled—both in conformity with the Beijing Rules and under the CRC—to have their privacy respected

---

[19] Art. 10 CCPR.
[20] Art. 15 CCPR.
[21] Art. 14(6) CCPR.
[22] CRC Committee, *Day of General Discussion* (note 2), para. 219. See also CRC Committee, *Concluding observations: China* (UN Doc. CRC/C/15/Add.56, 1996), para. 21.
[23] Guidelines for Action 16.

at all stages of the proceedings, including prior to the determination of criminal proceedings.

16. The omission of some of the safeguards found in other treaties, particularly the CCPR was not an oversight. The saving clause enshrined in Article 41 was intended to safeguard for children the protection of additional rights incorporated in other regional and international instruments. Had all the safeguards been repeated then there would have been a shifting in balance of the Convention away from persuading States to develop more child-oriented procedures to retaining procedures principally designed to protect adults with only minor modifications.

17. No one drafting the Convention foresaw its almost universal ratification. The non-repetition of certain standards may now cause difficulties for children living in States which although party to the CRC are not party to the CCPR.

18. Article 6 of the European Convention on Human Rights, which enshrines the main due process rights for those within the jurisdiction of the Council of Europe, does not contain any express reference to children. The only reference is to juveniles. The European Court of Human Rights however has not been hampered in its jurisprudence by limiting the protection to juveniles as defined by the Beijing Rules. The single protection offered to juveniles is that the press and the public may be excluded from all or part of the trial in the interests of the juvenile.

CHAPTER THREE

THE SCOPE OF ARTICLE 40

1. *Article 40(1)*

19. International law incorporates a number of basic principles upon which a child criminal justice system should be based. The first purpose is the encouragement of the well-being of children.[24] Both the CRC and the Beijing Rules emphasize the well-being of the child in the administration of child criminal justice.

20. The overriding right of the child to maintain regular personal relations and direct contact with his or her parents enshrined in Article 9(3) of the Convention, is one aspect of helping a child achieve this sense of well-being. The Beijing Rules specifically highlight the importance of maintaining the relationship with the child's family, so that the child is not treated in isolation from the family.[25]

The importance of maintaining family relationships is emphasized by the Guidelines for Action on Children in the Criminal Justice System which refer to the importance of ensuring easy access by relatives and persons who have a legitimate interest in the child where children are deprived of their liberty, unless the best interests of the child suggest otherwise.[26] In its concluding observations on the report of China, the CRC Committee expressed concern over the lack of access afforded to parents during the pre-trial detention of their children.[27] It is noticeable that the Guidelines give consideration to relationships over and above the family, referring to 'those with a legitimate interest in the child'. It also makes the proviso that such contact will only be justifiable if it is in the best interests of the child, which is in line with the approach of Article 9(3) of the UN Convention.

The CRC Committee also recognizes the importance of encouraging families to have closer and more frequent contact with children placed in

---

[24] Art. 40(4) CRC; Beijing Rule 5.
[25] Beijing Rule 1.1.
[26] Guidelines for Action 20.
[27] CRC Committee, *Concluding observations: China* (UN Doc. CRC/C/15/Add.56, 1996), para. 22.

institutions, and also to have a say in the child's treatment. One of the con-
clusions from the Day of Discussion was that, 'the child's socialisation should
be promoted through increasing the involvement of families in children's
programmes and through facilitating the release of children for home visit.'[28]

21. Another facet of promoting the child's sense of well-being is that in all
cases where children are 'alleged as, accused of, or recognized as having
infringed the penal law',[29] they should, according to the CRC, be treated in
a manner consistent with the promotion of their sense of dignity and worth,
and which reinforces their respect for human rights. Any treatment should
take into account the child's age and the desirability of promoting their
'reintegration' and their assumption of 'a constructive role in society.'[30]

22. After an intervention by the representative of the UN Centre for Social
Development and Humanitarian Affairs during the second reading of the
Convention, Article 40 does not incorporate the concept of a child's 'rehabilitation', which is defined as an aim of the administration of juvenile justice by Article 14(4) of the CCPR. The representative drew the attention of
States to the revision of thought which had occurred since the adoption of
the CCPR, and he highlighted the risk of States abusing rehabilitation as an
undesirable form of social control. It is also because the concept of rehabilitation implies that responsibility rests solely with an individual who can
be removed from society for treatment and once restored, released.

The use of 'Boot Camps' in the USA, a non-State Party to the Convention,
which adopt para-military style rehabilitation programmes, focusing on
rehabilitation rather than reintegration, appears to run contrary to the
objectives of institutional treatment set out in the Beijing Rules.

The notion of reintegration has a different starting point. It rejects the
assumption that the difficulties which children face are necessarily individual and considers the social environment of the child. Since the drafting of the CRC, the UN has adopted Guidelines for the Prevention of Juvenile
Delinquency[31] which seek to assist children develop a sense of responsibility and take the concept of integration further. Children should be assisted
within the community to develop a sense of responsibility which can only
be accomplished if the child begins to develop a sense of belonging. This

---

[28] CRC Committee, *Day of General Discussion* (note 2), para. 230.
[29] Art. 40(1) of the CRC.
[30] *Ibid.*
[31] UN Guidelines for the Prevention of Juvenile Delinquency (Riyadh Guidelines), adopted
and proclaimed by General Assembly resolution 45/112 of 14 December 1990.

poses the Human Rights Committee, which is the implementing body established by the CCPR, with a question. Should it continue to apply a standard which has since been rejected by the international community in a subsequent instrument? It is submitted that the Human Rights Committee should interpret the term 'rehabilitation' as the means by which a child can assume a constructive role in society. This ought certainly to be the case for States which are party both to the CCPR and the CRC and should from a teleological approach require non-CRC parties to take into account this new approach and to avoid the creation of two different standards.[32]

The CRC Committee may also be able to gain some assistance from approaches put forward in two of the regional human rights tribunals. In the case of Villagran Morales and others v Guatemala, the Inter-American Court stated that,[33]

> 'when the State apparatus has to intervene in offences committed by minors, it should make substantial efforts to guarantee their rehabilitation in order to allow them to play a constructive and productive role in society.'

While Judge Morenilla of the European Court, in his concurring opinion in the case of Nortier v The Netherlands, quoted from both the preamble and Article 40(3) of the CRC in order to state that the child criminal justice system should afford children,[34]

> '[...] the "necessary protection and assistance so that they can fully assume their responsibilities within the community," and prepare them "to live an individual life in society," by promoting "the establishment of laws, procedures, authorities and institutions applicable to children alleged as, accused of, or recognised as having infringed the penal law".'

2. Article 40(2)

Article 40(2)(a)

23. According to Article 40(2)(a) of the CRC, a child should not be accused or alleged to have infringed the penal law by reasons of acts or omissions which were not prohibited either by national or international law at the

---

[32] Art. 31(3) Vienna Convention on the Law of Treaties 1969.

[33] Inter-American Court of Human Rights, *Villagran Morales and others v Guatemala*, Judgment of 19 November 1999, Inter-Am. Ct. H.R. (Ser. C) No. 63 (1999)), para. 197.

[34] ECtHR, *Nortier v Netherlands*, Judgment (Merits) of 24 August 1993, application No. 13924/88, 17 EHRR 273, p. 291.

time that they were committed. The principle of non-retroactivity of the penal law is also enshrined in Article 15(1) of the CCPR, from which no derogation is permitted.[35]

Article 40(2)(b)(i)

24. Equally applicable to children and adults is the presumption of innocence. All children are presumed innocent until proven guilty according to law.

Article 40(2)(b)(ii)

25. When juveniles are apprehended, the Beijing Rules recommend that their parents or guardians should be notified 'immediately' or, if this is not possible, within the shortest possible time. The term 'guardians' is not restricted to legal guardians, but includes those who *de facto* have been responsible for the child. The recommended duty on a State to notify parents or guardians on the immediate apprehension of a juvenile is a higher standard than is found in treaty law. Article 9(4) of the CRC provides that where a child is separated from his or her family as a result of 'any action initiated by a State Party', essential information should be provided on request to family members on the whereabouts of the child, unless such information would be detrimental to the well-being of the child. However, this presupposes a request. Article 40(2)(b) of the CRC provides that the child should

> 'be informed promptly and directly of the charges against him or her and if appropriate through his or her parents or legal guardian and to have legal or other appropriate assistance in the preparation and presentation of his or her defence'

26. The duty placed on the State Party is only the duty to inform parents or guardians promptly of the charges. The CRC does not place a duty on the State Party to inform the parents or guardians at the earlier stage on the apprehension of the child before a charge is brought. Although Article 9(4) of the CRC is aimed at the major abuse of preventing disappearances, there appears to be a time gap between the operation of Article 9(4) and Article 40(2)(b)(ii), as there is only a duty to inform on request of the parents or once the authorities know the nature of the charge against the child. This was not the intention of the States drafting the Convention, as the situation was intended to have been covered by the chapeau to Article 40(2)(b):

---

[35] Art. 4(2) of the CCPR.

'Every child alleged as or accused of having infringed the penal law has at least the following guarantees [...]'. Unfortunately, the use of the word 'charges' in the original English language version appears to contradict this intention. The right of children, under binding international law, to have their parents notified of their immediate apprehension by law enforcement authorities, appears to have been sacrificed in the rush for the completion of the second reading of the CRC. Such a sacrifice will not assist in remedying the violations highlighted by the Defence for Children International report on children in adult prisons.[36]

27. The child's right to be informed promptly and directly of the charges is unqualified, as is the child's right to legal or other appropriate assistance in the preparation of his or her defence. The Fijian High Court in the case of Epeli Seniloli Anor v Semi Voliti, on behalf of Poasa Ravea Oawaoawa Voliti, awarded aggravated damages and punitive damages for false imprisonment where a 14 year-old who was handcuffed to a post at the police station after two items of food seized, was not told of the reasons for his arrest in contravention of Article 27 of the Constitution as well as the CRC.[37]

28. The right of a child to have his or her parents or legal guardians informed of the charges is qualified by the words 'if appropriate'. The qualification is introduced to protect the child's best interests. Where a child's best interest is not served by his or her parents being informed the State Party is entitled to exercise its discretion and withhold such information. In reaching such a decision, the State Party is under a duty to take into account the wishes of the child.

Article 40(2)(b)(iii)

29. Where a child's case has not been diverted away from juvenile justice fora, the child is entitled to have the matter determined by a 'competent independent and impartial authority or judicial body'.[38] Article 40 of the CRC incorporates the phrase 'authority or judicial body' to include all bodies of an a judicatory nature which have a responsibility in the juvenile justice field.[39]

---

[36] K. Tomasevski (ed.), *Children in Adult Prisons: An International Perspective* (London, Frances Printer, 1986). See further G. Van Bueren, *o.c.* (note 6), p. 176.

[37] High Court of Fiji, *Epeli Seniloli Anor v Semi Voliti*, Judgement of 22 February 2000, Civ. Appeal No. HBA 0033 of 1999 (unreported).

[38] Art. 40 (2)(iii) of the CRC.

[39] This includes the types of administrative boards which are found in Scotland and Scandinavia.

30. The emphasis is on the *'competent impartial and independent'* nature of the proceedings and hence under the CRC it is not essential that the body determining the charge is judicial, providing that the authority's procedures comply with the safeguards enshrined in the Convention.

The unusual and lengthy formulations found in Article 40(1) of the CRC ('States Parties recognise the right of every child alleged as, accused of, or recognised as having infringed the penal law') are intended to reflect the diversity in the types of juvenile proceedings throughout the world responsible for determining the penal responsibility of children. Even within industrialized States there is wide diversity. Scandinavian systems for the treatment of juvenile offenders developed from the poor laws, leaving as its inheritance a system of administrative bodies, whereas in the United States the treatment of juveniles evolved from the adult court system.[40] Amongst developing States some have neither juvenile courts nor at a national level specific legislation on juvenile offenders. Juveniles are tried in the same courts and under the same legislation as adults although the sentence may be reduced on account of age. Others such as Bolivia have established juvenile courts, juvenile homes for those under 16 and specially trained police corps for dealing with children.

Both the CRC and the Beijing Rules recognize that non-judicial bodies are not considered incompatible with international human rights law providing the hearings are fair according to law. Defence for Children International, however, takes this one step further arguing that 'it would be difficult if not impossible for a tribunal which does not include a trained judge or magistrate to meet this requirement.'[41]

In a number of States where juvenile courts either do not exist or are found only in the larger urban areas, criminal courts have jurisdiction over juvenile offences. However, where criminal courts are applying juvenile codes, the practice of a number of States reveals a tendency for the judges to apply juvenile law 'in a way which is strongly coloured by the outlook of a criminal judge' and without paying heed to the child's developmental

---

[40] Although the two systems are different they both were developed in the 1890's. The Child Welfare Act of Sweden (1965) Trans. Ministry of Justice. See also the work and make-up of Children's Panels, Social Work (Scotland) Act (1968) and contrast this with the *juge des enfants* in M. King and C. Piper, *How the Law thinks about Children* (Aldershot, Ashgate Publishing, 1990).

[41] D. O'Donnell, *Juvenile Justice and the Rights of the Child: a paper prepared for the Seminar on Human Rights and Juvenile Justice, Barbados, 1989* (Geneva, Defence for Children International, 1989).

entitlements.[42] The Guidelines for Action on Children in the Criminal Justice System[43] refer to the need for a child-centred criminal justice process which should establish youth courts. Alternatively, regular courts should incorporate such procedures as appropriate.[44] In examining States Parties reports under Article 40, the CRC Committee will need to consider whether and to what degree States which rely on the criminal courts are fulfilling their duty to take into account the child's age and desirability of promoting the child's reintegration. In examining States Parties' reports under Article 40, the CRC Committee has regularly commented on the failure of States to take into account the child's age and desirability of promoting the child's reintegration. The report of the Secretary-General on the Administration of Justice referred to concerns that were commonly raised by the Committee. These included the incompatibility of domestic laws with the CRC, the absence or insufficient numbers of judges who have received training on the relevant international standards, and the insufficient legal protection and resources allocated to the psychological recovery and social reintegration of child offenders.[45]

31. The CRC, the CCPR, the regional human rights treaties, and the Beijing Rules provide a framework for applying the principles of natural justice to children, many of which are equally applicable to adults. The CRC states clearly that the Convention lays down only the minimum of guarantees. Article 40 (2)(b) provides that a child has 'at least the following guarantees'. The implication of this is that protections which are included in other international and regional human rights treaties are also applicable to children.

Children, like adults, benefit from the *principle of equality* before the law. All persons are equal before the courts and tribunals, in both the determination of criminal cases and civil rights and obligations. A child is entitled, according to Article 40(2)(b)(iii) of the CRC,

> 'to have the matter determined without delay by a competent independent and impartial authority or judicial body in a fair hearing according to law, in the presence of legal or other appropriate assistance unless it is considered

---

[42] *Ibid.*
[43] *Cf. supra* note 3.
[44] Guidelines for Action 14.
[45] Secretary-General, *Human rights in the administration of justice, in particular of children and juveniles in detention: Report to the Commission on Human Rights* (UN Doc. E/CN.4/2002/63, 2002), para. 20.

not to be in the best interest of the child, in particular taking into account his or her age or situation, his or her parents or legal guardians.'

In re Gault, the United States Supreme Court concluded that some due process rights do not endanger the informality and aims of rehabilitation which characterize juvenile proceedings. At a minimum, juveniles are entitled to adequate notice and time to prepare a defence, right to counsel, right to cross-examination, and self incrimination guarantees.[46] However, juveniles in the United States have not been granted the right to trial by jury.[47]

The fair trial rights of a child charged with an offence were considered in two concurring opinions in the case of Nortier v Netherlands which was heard before the European Court of Human Rights. Judge Walsh stated in his concurring opinion that,[48]

> '[j]uveniles facing criminal charges and trial are as fully entitled as adults to benefit from all the Convention requirements for a fair trial. Great care must be taken to ensure that this entitlement is not diluted by considerations of rehabilitation and reform. These are considerations which should be in addition to all the procedural protections available. Fair trial and proper proof of guilt are absolute conditions precedent.'

In his concurring opinion, Judge Morenilla referred to Article 25 of the Universal Declaration of Human Rights as well as the CRC in order to highlight that the child should be entitled to additional protection beyond the guarantees set out in the European Convention. He took the view that,[49]

> '[...] minors are entitled to the same protection of their fundamental rights as adults but that their developing state of personality—and consequently their limited social responsibility—should be taken into account in applying article 6 of the Convention. In particular, the right of everyone charged with a criminal offence to be judged by an impartial tribunal should not be incompatible with the protective treatment of juvenile offenders.'

This approach can be distinguished from criticisms levelled at the United States for merely transposing adult fair trial rights on to child offenders.[50]

---

[46] United States Supreme Court, *In re Gault* (387 US 1, 1967). Juvenile courts are also under a duty to apply the criminal standard of proof: see United States Supreme Court, *In re Winship* (397 US 358, 1970).

[47] United States Supreme Court, *McKeiver v Pennsylvania* (403 US 528, 1970).

[48] ECtHR, *Nortier v Netherlands* (note 34), p. 290.

[49] *Ibid.*, p. 291.

[50] E. Buss, 'The Missed Opportunity in Gault', *University of Chicago Law Review*, No. 70, 2003, p. 39.

32. For children in the jurisdiction of States Parties to the CRC, the matter is to be determined *'without delay'*. The same emphasis on speed is found in Article 10(2)(b) of the CCPR, which entitles juveniles to be brought 'as speedily as possible for judication' and, which, according to the Human Rights Committee, is an unconditional duty on States Parties and is therefore not dependant upon the States Parties' resources.[51] In K v Lord Advocate, the Privy Council found that a breach of the right to a fair trial had occurred where a period of 27–28 months had elapsed in bringing the case to trial for no justifiable reason. The Privy Council stated that when dealing with children, the time requirement in the European Convention had to be read in the light of the CRC and the Beijing Rules.[52]

33. The child's right to the presence of legal or other appropriate assistance enshrined in Article 40(2)(b)(iii) is qualified by the phrase, *'unless it is not considered to be in the interest of the child'* so as to take into account the more informal approaches to juvenile justice which some States have adopted. In Scotland, children may be deprived of their liberty for up to seven days prior to attending a children's hearing. The children and their families do have access to lawyers during this period but legal representation is not available at the proceedings of the children's hearings themselves.[53]

Overemphasis should not necessarily be placed on legal or non-legal qualifications of the child's representative; it is the quality of the representation which is important. This does not necessarily imply that the role of the juvenile's representative ought to be the same as an adult's defence counsel, but that the child has to feel confident that there is an informed and well-trained independent professional on whom the child can rely both for advice and representation. Nevertheless, cognisance ought to be taken of a UNITAR study which found that the right to counsel can become more important for children because of the informality of juvenile proceedings. There is a risk that such informality can unwittingly lead to an absence of adherence to the required international procedural safeguards.[54]

---

[51] Human Rights Committee, *General Comment No. 9: Humane treatment of persons deprived of liberty (Art. 10)*(UN Doc. HRI/GEN/Rev.7, 2004), para. 2, which was confirmed in Human Rights Committee, *General Comment No. 21: Humane treatment of persons deprived of liberty (Art. 10)*(UN Doc. HRI/GEN/Rev.7, 2004), para. 13.

[52] United Kingdom Privy Council, *K v Lord Advocate* (4 LRC 577, 2002).

[53] See the reservation of the United Kingdom to Art. 37(d) by which it 'reserves its rights to continue the present operation of children's panels'.

[54] A.M. Pappas, 'Law and the Status of the Child LII–LIII', *Columbia Journal Human Rights Review*, No. 13, 1981.

Whether the proceedings are formal or informal, they shall be conducive to the best interests of the juvenile and shall be conducted in an atmosphere of understanding, which shall allow the juvenile to participate therein and to express herself or himself freely.[55]

34. This provision has been strengthened by Article 12(2) of the CRC, which places States Parties under a duty to provide children with an opportunity to be heard in any judicial or administrative proceeding affecting the child

> 'either directly, or through a representative or an appropriate body, in a manner consistent with the procedural rules of national law'.

The reference to the national procedural laws qualifies only the method of participation, whether directly or through a representative. It was not intended to restrict the child's right to participate. The framework of both the CRC and the Beijing Rules provides an opportunity for States to consider thoroughly juvenile trials and hearings from the perspective of child participation. Such an approach needs to consider not only the admissibility of evidence but also all aspects of the environment of such proceedings.

35. Article 14(2)(d) of the CCPR also provides for both adults and children the right

> 'to be tried in his presence and to defend himself in person or through legal assistance of his own choosing to be informed if he does not have legal assistance of this right and to have legal assistance assigned to him in any case where the interests of justice so require and without payment by him in any such case if he does not have sufficient means to pay for it'

36. Both the CRC and the Beijing Rules provide for the participation of the child's parents or guardians in the proceedings, as their presence can provide a child with support and helpful emotional assistance. However, the State is entitled to withhold its consent to parental participation where it does not consider it to be in the child's best interest. For States Parties to the CRC both participation and non-participation should be based on the child's consent.

Although the Beijing Rules are non-binding, Rule 7(1) comprehensively sets out the basic procedural safeguards. The list is non-exhaustive as the words 'such as' precede the following list: the presumption of innocence, the right to be notified of the charges, the right to remain silent, the right to counsel, the right to the presence of a parent or guardian the right to

---

[55] Beijing Rule 14(2).

confront and cross examine witnesses, and the right to appeal to a higher authority shall be guaranteed at all stages of proceedings.

Article 40(2)(b)(iv)

37. An additional safeguard for children is found only in the Beijing Rules. Beijing Rule 7 recommends that children should be entitled to the right to silence as a 'basic procedural safeguard'. Children may be more vulnerable to pressures to 'confess' and the right to silence helps to prevent such pressures. The protection in both the CRC and the CCPR does not appear to be as extensive. The CRC only provides that a child should, 'not be compelled to give testimony or to confess guilt' and the CCPR prohibition is expressed in similar terms. An individual may not be compelled to give testimony or to confess guilt but under the CCPR and the CRC it would appear that adverse inferences could be drawn from silence and refusal to answer questions whilst in custody. This is particularly important for children, as the Defence for Children International study[56] pointed to the abuses which occurred whilst children were in police custody. The potential of such a safeguard is highlighted by the General Comments of the Human Rights Committee which, in commenting generally on the rules of evidence, observed that national laws should ensure that any evidence which is acquired in breach of international human rights law should not be regarded as admissible by the courts. Unless States incorporate the Beijing Rules into their own legislation, there will not be any binding legal duty on them to acknowledge the additional facets of the right of silence.

Article 40(2)(b)(v) and (vi)

38. They are standards, with the exception of the right to the presence of parents and right to remain silent, which apply to both adults and children, and which are found in existing binding instruments. Children equally have the right to examine witnesses, and where children are found guilty of having infringed the criminal law, they are entitled to have both their conviction and sentence reviewed by a higher tribunal according to law. As with adults, where children cannot understand or speak the language used, they are entitled to the free assistance of an interpreter. In a new application of the interpretation requirement in Kwa Zulu Natal in South Africa, child

---

[56] *Cf. supra* note 36.

victims of sex abuse are not asked questions directly by a counsel. Rather, the questions are put to the interpreter, and only if the interpreter can understand the question, the latter will be put to the child.

It is also arguable that the same need for child centred proceedings should apply to review or appeal proceedings where the child is in court for that review or appeal proceeding. This extends to the need for specific child rights training for those lawyers and judges conducting the appeal.

Article 40(2)(b)(vii)

39. Article 40 (2)(b)(vii) of the CRC places a duty on States Parties to guarantee to children their right to privacy at all stages of the proceedings. One aspect of this right is highlighted by the CCPR, which allows for the public to be excluded from juvenile justice proceedings and for the judgement not to be made public. Such proceedings include matrimonial disputes concerning the guardianship of children. Van Nijnatten argues that decisions which have profound consequences for the lives of children and their families ought to be open to public scrutiny.[57] This is a forceful argument which child advocates have to confront. Any exception to the principle of open justice can only be sustained by reliance upon the best interests of the child. With open proceedings, the chances of the child being stigmatized would increase and the informality would decrease. However, there is a danger that in human rights cases, violations may go unnoticed in proceedings not open to the public.

40. Another facet of the right to privacy is highlighted by the Beijing Rules, which recommend in principle that information leading to the identification of a juvenile offender should not be published.[58] Such information would include, but is not limited to, the name. This protects the child's right to privacy and serves to prevent children from being identified or labelled as delinquents as criminological research has shown such labelling has had detrimental effects on children. The CRC clearly provides that the child's right to privacy should be 'fully respected' at all stages in the proceedings and it is arguably implicit in the right to privacy that a child should not be identified. In V v UK, the applicant complained that the public nature of

---

[57] C. van Nijnatten, 'Behind Closed Door: Juvenile Hearings in the Netherlands', *International Journal of Law and the Family* 3, 1989, p. 177.
[58] Beijing Rule 8(2).

criminal proceedings against a twelve year-old that took place over three weeks in public in an adult Crown Court, violated his rights under Article 3 of the European Convention. The European Court recognized that one of the minimum guarantees provided by Article 40(2)(b) of the CRC is that children accused of crimes should have their privacy respected at all stages of the proceedings. It also made reference to Rule 8 of the Beijing Rules and noted the Committee of Ministers recommendation in 1987 that member States should review their law and practice with a view to avoiding committing minors to adult courts where Juvenile courts exist and to recognising right to respect their private lives.[59] The Court did not find a violation. It stated that [60]

> '[E]ven if there is evidence that the proceedings would have a harmful effect on an eleven year old—psychiatric evidence before the trial was that V suffered post-traumatic effects of the offence and cried inconsolably throughout, found it difficult to talk about what he and T had done and suffered fears of punishment and terrible retribution. The Court is not convinced that the particular features of the trial process caused him suffering beyond which would have inevitably been engendered in dealing with the matter.'

The Court could be criticized here for choosing to gloss over the particular detriment that the public nature of the trial had on V's well being, by determining that he would have inevitably suffered by having to go through the trial process. In doing so, the Court compromised the principle of privacy on the basis of other facts before it. The Court did not respect the right of the child to have his privacy fully respected under Article 40(2)(b)(vii) of the CRC. This has had the effect of eroding the right from a minimum guarantee to merely a factor to be taken into account when determining where to strike the balance between the child's right to privacy and the media's reporting freedom.[61] This contradicts the evolving and dynamic approach that is supposed to be given to the interpretation of European Convention provisions.

The right to privacy of child offenders may be said to have ramifications which extend beyond their childhood. In Venables v News Group Newspapers, the boys who killed James Bulger were granted lifelong anonymity. This

---

[59] ECtHR, *V v UK*, Judgment (Merits and just satisfaction) of 16 December 1999, application No 24888/94, Reports of Judgments and Decisions 1999-IX, 30 EHRR 121, (hereinafter: ECtHR, *V v UK*), para. 76.
[60] *Ibid.*, para. 79.
[61] New Zealand High Court, *R v F* (22 June 1999).

decision reflected their status as children when they were sentenced, although the decision was primarily concerned with the extent of the threat to their lives if their identities were ever revealed.[62]

41. It is interesting to note the value which the European Court attributed to the other international law standards that it considered when determining the question of privacy in V v UK. On the one hand, it recognized that such instruments should be taken into consideration where they demonstrated a trend in the manner in which a Convention right is to be protected. However, the Court concluded that it cannot be determinative of the question.[63] The Beijing Rules would be unlikely to be of any more than subsidiary support, save to the extent that they might provide the Court with some guidance on the perimeters of a particular right.

Their value was also recognized in the case of S v Kwalese, where the South African Cape Provincial Division saw the information contained in the rules and its commentary as being 'particularly significant'.[64] However, this approach must be assessed in light of the South African constitutional position which obliges courts to consider all international law, regardless of whether binding or not.

The importance of the Beijing Rules has been acknowledged in the UN resolutions on the administration of child criminal justice and by the CRC Committee when commenting on the reports of State Parties.[65] It may well be that the Beijing Rules have their most decisive impact when considered along with other international standards in criminal policy discussions and in legislation.[66]

42. The duty on States Parties also extends to privacy of records. The details are usefully set out in the non-binding Beijing Rules but, in substance, they form a part of the child's right to privacy, which is found in binding treaty form. States Parties are under a duty to keep records of juvenile offenders 'strictly confidential' and inaccessible to third parties. Access to such records

---

[62] High Court of England and Wales, *Venables v News Group Newspapers* (8 January 2001). See also Mary Bell's case in which continued anonymity was also granted in order to protect the right to private and family life which she shared with her daughter.

[63] ECtHR, *V v UK* (note 59), para. 77.

[64] South African Cape Provincial Division, *S v Kwalese* (2000 (2) SACR 135), p. 139.

[65] *E.g.* CRC Committee, *Concluding observations: Mongolia* (UN Doc. CRC/C/15/Add.48, 1996), para. 29.

[66] See O. Bonke, *The Application of the United Nations Standards and Norms in Crime Prevention and Criminal Justice: Expert Group Meeting, Austria 10-12 February 2003* (Vienna, UN Office on Drugs and Crime, 2003), p. 49.

should be limited to those individuals who are directly concerned with the case. Finally, Beijing Rule 21(2) also provides that where a juvenile is subsequently involved in adult proceedings, the records of any juvenile proceedings should be inadmissible.

3. *Article 40(3)*

43. As a means of fulfilling the aims of child criminal justice enshrined in international law, Article 40(3) of the CRC provides that States Parties should seek,

> 'to promote the establishment of laws, procedures, authorities and institutions specifically applicable to children [...]'

44. This is an important addition to the protection of the rights of children who are accused of being in conflict with the law as Article 14(4) of the CCPR is far more limited and only provides that procedures concerning juveniles should 'take into account their age and the desirability of promoting rehabilitation.' Under the CRC, States Parties are under a duty to 'seek to promote the establishment of' specific procedures and institutions dealing separately with children'. However, the duty in the American Convention on Human Rights is stricter and more direct. These provisions recognize that a separate child criminal justice system can be attuned to the specific needs of children and can better ensure successful reintegration.[67]

Where separate systems of justice are established, they should still be in conformity with international human rights law. The CRC places a duty on States Parties to maintain a balance between the informality of proceedings and the protection of the fundamental rights of the child. Regardless of whether law enforcement officials are in specific child institutions or not, Rule 10(3) of the Beijing Rules recommends that all law officials who come into contact with children, should 'avoid harm to her or him with due regard to the circumstances of the case.' In defining the avoidance of harm, the Beijing Commentary specifically cites as examples 'the use of harsh language, physical violence or exposure to the environment'. The Beijing Rules' prohibition of 'harm' is broader than the customary prohibition of torture, cruel, inhuman and degrading treatment and punishment. Both the Beijing Rules and the CRC are based on the principle that any involvement in the

---

[67] Art. 5(5).

child criminal justice system can be 'harmful' *per se,* even though—as the Beijing Commentary points out—compassion and kind firmness ought to be important elements in any such process.

45. Another basic principle enshrined in international law is that the concept of criminal responsibility should be related to the age at which children are able to understand the consequences of their actions. The CRC places a duty on States Parties to 'seek to promote' the establishment of a minimum age below which children should be presumed not to have the capacity to infringe the penal law. The CRC Committee has highlighted the failure of certain States Parties to establish such a minimum age of criminal responsibility. Inevitably, when establishing minimum ages there is arbitrariness, but the Beijing Rules endeavour to provide guidance for States when exercising their discretion, in linking the minimum age for criminal responsibility to the child's development and maturity. Rule 4 of the Beijing Rules recommends that when States establish an age of criminal responsibility,

> 'the beginning of that age shall not be fixed at too low an age level bearing in mind the facts of emotional mental and intellectual maturity.'

The question of establishing a minimum age for criminal responsibility differs widely 'owing to history and culture'. But, as the Beijing Commentary points out, if the age of criminal responsibility were too low or non-existent, then the concept of responsibility would become meaningless. This point received support through the dicta in a South African Court presiding over a case in which a ten year-old boy was charged with the indecent assault of an eight year-old girl. Judge Greenland held that [68]

> '[t]hough mindful of the Attorney-General's prerogative in regard to prosecutions, I am compelled to hold it is wrong, unjust and prejudicial to the interests of the accused and society to prosecute a child where the evidence is that such child will not understand or appreciate the proceedings.'

Paradoxically, although there is an arbitrariness in setting a minimum age, the choice must not be arbitrary. The CRC Committee has called upon countries to raise the minimum age of responsibility.[69] It has also on occasion recommended that certain countries give serious consideration to reviewing their minimum ages with a view to raising them.[70]

---

[68] *S v F 1* ((1989) SA 460 (ZH)), p. 462.

[69] See for example CRC Committee, *Concluding observations: Australia* (UN Doc. CRC/C/15/Add.79, 1997), *India* (UN Doc. CRC/C15/Add.115, 2000), *Fiji* (UN Doc. CRC/C15/Add.89, 1998), *United Kingdom of Great Britain and Northern Ireland* (UN Doc. CRC/C/15/Add.34, 1995), *Barbados* (UN Doc. CRC/C15/Add.103, 1999).

[70] See CRC Committee, *Concluding observations: Belize* (UN Doc. CRC/C/15/Add.99, 1999),

The Committee has not taken the initiative of establishing a universal minimum age of criminal responsibility. The Committee may well feel inhibited by the lack of consensus with respect to the appropriate minimum age, in addition to a reluctance to impose on the religious or cultural traditions that may have influenced the setting of the age. However, it is not helpful in seeking to move towards consistency when it criticizes the minimum age of 10 in England as Wales as being unlawful, while only recommending that Ireland, which had just raised the minimum age from 7 to 10, only consider reviewing the age with a view to an increasing it.

At present there is a wide disparity in the minimum age, not only globally but also in the same continent. This raises the question whether children mature at such different paces even within the same continent.[71] However, the opportunity to limit the arbitrariness of the minimum age of criminal responsibility for member States of the Council of Europe was passed up by the majority of the European Court of Human Rights in the case of V v UK. The Court was faced with the argument that the low minimum age of responsibility amounted to inhuman and degrading treatment under Article 3 of the European Convention. The Court appreciated that it is well-established in its case law that the Convention is a living instrument and must take account of the standards prevailing amongst member States of the Council of Europe.[72] It was also highlighted that the CRC Committee had been very critical of the age set in England and Wales. However, the Court also observed that there was no commonly accepted minimum age for the imposition of criminal responsibility in relevant international texts or in Europe. While the age set was at the low end of the scale, other countries in Europe had adopted a younger age of criminal responsibility.[73] Accordingly, the Court did not consider that there was at this stage any clear common standard among member States of the Council of Europe. However, as cases on adult trans-sexuality demonstrate, the European Court of Human Rights is cogniscent of changing trends and the decision on the minimum age of criminal responsibility in V and T may be ripe for reopening.

46. The desirability of diverting children away from formal trial procedures is another principle which is incorporated into the CRC. A diversion is the utilisation of formal or informal means other than the criminal justice

---

Ireland (UN Doc. CRC/C/15/Add.85, 1998) and *Trinidad and Tobago* (UN Doc. CRC/C/15/Add.82, 1997).

[71] G. Van Bueren, 'Child Oriented Justice—An International Challenge for Europe', *International Journal of Law and the Family* 6, 1992, (381) p. 387.

[72] ECtHR, *V v UK* (note 59)(31 EHRR 121), para. 72.

[73] *Ibid.*, para. 73.

system to deal with young offenders. Diversions are one aspect of promoting the child's sense of well-being, as it avoids the negative effects of child criminal justice proceedings, including the stigma of conviction and sentence. It also provides a route through which arrest, detention or imprisonment can be avoided in accordance with Article 37(b) of the CRC. Diversions may be used at any stage and are not necessarily limited to minor offences. They therefore have great potential and practical scope. In one sense, however, the term diversions is misleading as children are not diverted away from the legal system itself but merely from its more formal aspects.

47. The Beijing Rules provide that appropriate consideration should be given for dealing with juvenile offenders without resorting to formal trial. The Beijing Commentary notes that in many cases non-intervention would be the best response, and diversion at the outset without referral to alternative social services may be the optimal response. Such responses include counselling, community service and restitution to the victim. A similar policy has been adopted by the Council of Europe. The Council of Europe Recommendation on Social Reactions to Juvenile Delinquency encourages the development of diversion and mediation procedures both at public prosecutor level by the discontinuance of proceedings and at the police level.[74] Although the recommendations of the Council of Europe are not legally binding they are adopted unanimously and so carry weight and indicate a common approach to policy and minimum standards.[75] These standards have now been reinforced by Article 40(3)(b) of the CRC, which places States Parties under to a duty to seek to promote,

> 'whenever appropriate and desirable measures for dealing with such children without resorting to judicial proceedings, providing that human rights and legal safeguards are fully respected.'

The final clause is very important. Diversionary methods can only be implemented in a manner consistent with a child's human rights and legal safeguards. Consequently it is a fundamental principle of diversions that referral to appropriate community or other services should require the consent of the child and where appropriate the consent of his or her parents or guardians. This is a principle equally applicable to adults as without the consent forced community service could breach Article 1(a) of International Labour Organisation Convention No. 105 Concerning the Abolition of Forced Labour 1957. The 1997 Guidelines for Action on Children in Criminal Justice

---

[74] Council of Europe Recommendation 84(10), adopted on 17 September 1987.
[75] See also Council of Europe Recommendations (92)16, (99)19 and (2000)20.

System states in Guideline 15 that 'A review of existing procedures should be undertaken and, where possible, diversion or other alternative initiatives should be developed to avoid recourse to the criminal justice system for young persons.'

Because diversions depend on the consent of the individual, Beijing Rule 11(3) recommends that consent to a diversion should be subject to review by a competent authority upon application. The provision for such a safeguard is to protect children from consenting to a diversion because they feel coerced and wish to avoid a court appearance.

The Beijing Rules also provide guidance to States seeking to make diversions an effective and attractive option. The police and prosecution agencies should be empowered to dispose of such cases at their discretion in accordance both with their legal systems and with the principles contained in the Beijing Rules.

48. The development of minimum standards and guidelines for diversion programmes would assist in raising the profile of diversionary measures among States. While the discretion to use diversionary measures would remain with prosecution agencies, the establishment of minimum standards might assist in ensuring that the measures are not used in an arbitrary manner.

The Beijing Rules recommend that States should make efforts to provide for community programmes such as temporary supervision and guidance, restitution and compensation of victims. One partial consequence of the promotion of diversion has been the increasing emphasis being placed on the value of restorative justice programmes with respect to child offenders. Restorative justice is a process by which the parties affected by a specific offence can sit down in order to try and establish a way to repair the harm that has been done. This may be through, for example, monetary repayment, an apology or community service. The restorative justice process has a number of potential benefits. It is relatively inexpensive and eases the burden on criminal justice systems. It provides a way in which young offenders have to face the victims of crime and recognize the effects their actions will have had on another. It also means that child offenders will not have the stigma of convictions on their records.

The process also has considerable advantages for the victim of the crime. It allows that person the opportunity to play a central role in determining the punishment for a crime, which may be more empowering than attending court where the victim's role is often limited to that of a witness with no say in the sentence passed. Victims may also feel that restorative justice helps them to re-establish their dignity and to draw a line under their 'victim' status.[76] The UN Handbook on Justice for Victims highlights that 'the framework for restorative justice involves, the offender, the victim and the entire community in efforts to create a balanced approach that is offender-directed and, at the same time, victim-centred'.

49. Family Group Conferencing programmes may be particularly beneficial in bringing the offender, the victim and their families into the diversion process. Family members involvement will usually be encouraged, so long as it is of benefit to the child offender. The Guidelines for Action on Children in the Criminal Justice System refer in Guideline 15 to the use of the family in diversion mechanisms. During the Discussion Day on Juvenile Justice, the CRC Committee has also acknowledged the importance attached by traditional systems to the family, including the extended family, as well as to the community in the process of ensuring social reintegration and promoting their active participation in society.

4. Article 40(4)

50. Article 40(4) places a duty on States Parties to make available a wide variety of dispositions as alternatives to institutional care. The breadth of the choices is to ensure that a State does not follow a 'one size fits all' approach as the diversionary procedures are required to suit the entitlements of each individual child. There is the risk that diversions may be adopted as being regarded as a cheap alternative to institutional punishments. However, this is not necessarily the case. Foster placement, for example, which is expressly listed as a diversionary disposition requires very careful State support and monitoring as the opportunities for abuse are well documented.[77] The importance that the UN places on such alternatives is clear from the fact that the principle is followed by a, for a treaty, comparably lengthy list citing examples of a wide range of alternatives to custody. This list is followed by both a justification and a guiding principle for States Parties that any disposition should be appropriate to the child's well-being and proportionate to the child's circumstances and the offence.

---

[76] H. Strang, 'Justice for Victims of Young Offender: The Centrality of Emotional Harm and Restoration' in G. Johnstone (ed.), *A Restorative Justice Reader* (Devonshire, Willan Publishing, 2003).

[77] See further Van Bueren, *o.c.* (note 6), p. 103.

The Guidelines for Action on Children in the Criminal Justice System asserts that efforts should be made to establish and apply programmes aimed at strengthening social assistance which would allow for diversion.[78] The CRC Committee endorsed the value of diversionary mechanisms when urging the Russian Federation to make wider use of alternatives to deprivation of liberty, and to make the necessary resources available for administering such alternatives.[79] Such diversions, however, can only occur after a child has admitted guilt. It is contrary to international law to use any diversionary procedures as pressure for a child to admit an offence which he or she did not commit.

---

[78] Guidelines for Action 42.
[79] CRC Committee, *Concluding observations: Russian Federation* (UN Doc. CRC/C/Add.110, 1999), para. 70.